MY
NEW
SUPERPOWER

And Other Stories
We Write Together

ONCE UPON A PANCAKE
Making Reading and Writing Fun

MY NEW SUPERPOWER

And Other Stories We Write Together

STARTED BY RICK BENGER

Collins

An imprint of HarperCollins*Publishers*Ltd

WRITTEN BY

THAT'S YOU! ↗
WRITE YOUR NAMES

STARTED BY **Rick Benger**

LEAD ILLUSTRATION BY **Maddie Egremont**

EDITED BY **Karin Fisher-Golton**

COVER DESIGN BY **Zeena Baybayan**

A NOTE FOR GROWN-UPS

This book is suitable for children of ages 6–8 (or so), who are typically learning to read and write. You'll help by doing the bulk of the reading and writing, to keep the stories going and the creativity flowing. It's best to transcribe word-for-word, so the children can fully experience the power of their own storytelling. Don't worry about tying the stories up with beginnings, middles, and ends—the joy is in setting the imagination free and capturing creativity on the page.

The real magic begins when you take turns to imagine what happens next. It helps to use different colors for each storyteller, e.g. red for Maria, green for Harry, blue for Mom.

HAVE FUN!
RICK

P.S. For finished story examples and other creative inspiration, take a peek at our Instagram (@uponapancake) and website (onceuponapancake.com).

Hazel was reading a wonderful book called ....
....

She was very tired but wanted to keep reading. She kept her eyes open as long as she could, which wasn't long. She fell asleep and started to dream about ....

....
....
....
....
....
....
....
....

DRAW HAZEL'S DREAM

....
....
....
....

STORY #1

WHAT HAPPENED
WHEN HAZEL
WOKE UP?

STORY #1

Of all the superpowers, I got a silly one—the ability to

....

....

But a silly superpower isn't going to stop me from being awesome. And that means I need an awesome costume.

DRAW THE
COSTUME!

I finish creating my costume and put it on. Perfect. Time to really try out my new superpower.

HOW?
WHERE?

KEEP GOING . . .

... CONTINUED

IS ANYBODY ELSE INVOLVED? GOOD GUYS? BAD GUYS?

DRAW WHAT
HANDS!

STORY #2

Nathan is hungry. He opens the fridge and *SPLAT*, something greasy hits him in the face.

"Get down!" says a squeaky little voice.

"What . . . who said that!?" says Nathan.

"Me!"

Nathan sees that a tiny elf is speaking. The elf is hiding behind the butter dish, making little butter-balls.

It's the final soccer game of the season, and Sara is full of worry.

Usually, Jayden plays goalkeeper. But Jayden is sick, and the coach picked Sara to take his place.

The other team kicks off the first half. Then

WHAT DOES SARA DO?

STORY #4

Olivia has exactly 17 minutes and 21 seconds to save the galaxy. Yikes.

First, she has to figure out what happened. She looks around the spaceship control deck for clues.

WHAT DOES
SHE NOTICE?

WHERE DID THE
CAPTAIN GO?

KEEP GOING . . .

... CONTINUED

6 MINUTES AND
42 SECONDS
LEFT!

UH-OH. ONLY 30
SECONDS TO GO!

Lucas the little puff of wind doesn't want to leave his cloud and start the day.

"I'm too tired to get up!" he tells his parents.

"But what about the sailboats?" they ask. "Without you, how will they move across the bay?"

"I'm just a little puff. I can't move them much."

"What about the fuzzy balls on the dandelions? How will they float away and find new places to grow?"

"I'm just a tiny breeze," says Lucas. "I won't help them much."

"What about

....

....

....

....

....

....

....

....

....

....

....

....

DOES LUCAS
GET UP FROM
HIS CLOUD?

My friends and I are playing Hide and Seek. I'm It.
    I finish counting and call out, "Ready or not, here I come!"

    It's easy to find Tony the Turtle. He is near the ....

....

    Next I find ....

....

....

....

....

....

....

....

....

....

....

KEEP GOING . . .

FIVE FRIENDS TO FIND! LOOK FOR A TURTLE,
A TOUCAN, A JAGUAR, A MONKEY, AND A CHAMELEON.
(HINT: THE CHAMELEON LOOKS LIKE THIS 🦎.)

STORY #7

...CONTINUED

FOUND THEM ALL?
NOW WHAT HAPPENS?

STORY #7

Fatima's favorite store is called Quirk & Quirk's Old Stuff and Thingamabobs. Everything inside is old, rare, or downright weird.

One afternoon, Fatima walks by Quirk & Quirk's and sees something new in the window—a can of rainbow paint. Cool! She walks in and buys the can.

WHAT DOES
FATIMA PAINT?

STORY #8

WHAT HAPPENS
WHEN SHE FINISHES
PAINTING?

"I told you not to go to the top of Muddle Mountain," says Grandma Lion. "Remember? I said you'd get . . . "

"Mixed up!" says Baby Giraffe.

"Messed up!" says Baby Elephant.

"Muddled up!" says Baby Ostrich.

"Exactly," says Grandma Lion. "But I can see you went up there anyway. Just look at you! Your tops and bottoms are all switched around!"

STORY #9

KEEP GOING...

DRAW THE BABY
ANIMALS!

STORY #9

...CONTINUED

DO THE
BABY ANIMALS
GET UNMUDDLED?

Marco wakes up to perfect Saturday weather—rain.
Rain means his parents won't make him go outside
and play. He can stay inside all day and invent things.

He reaches under his bed, pulls out his box of treasures,
and dumps everything on the floor.

WHICH TREASURES
DOES MARCO USE?

WHAT DOES
MARCO DO WITH
HIS INVENTION?

STORY #10

I was playing basketball with .... WHO? ↙

when I heard a deep rumble and a loud buzz. I looked around. There was a spaceship landing at the other end of the court.

Its door went *whoosh* and out came some aliens, cool and casual, as though it was no big deal.

They didn't look like you'd expect.

....

....

....

DESCRIBE
THE ALIENS

....

....

....

Then one of them said, " ....

....

....

....

....

....

....

....

STORY #11

In Maya's house, there was a big old grandfather clock.

TICK, its pendulum swung to the left.

TOCK, its pendulum swung to the right.

TICK, TOCK went the old grandfather clock—until it stopped.

It stopped between a TICK and a TOCK, and the whole world stopped too.

Maya's dad froze mid-sneeze, between the AH and the CHOO.

Maya's dog froze mid-bark, between the BOW and the WOW.

But Maya didn't freeze. Time had stopped but not for her.

WHAT HAPPENED
WHEN TIME
STOPPED?

KEEP GOING . . .

... CONTINUED

DID TIME START
AGAIN? HOW?

Mike was getting bored of Halloween, mainly because his mom always made him go trick-or-treating with his little sister.

But free candy was free candy. So Mike went along, dressed up as

....

....

His sister dressed up as

....

....

It was a successful night. Mike's bag was full, and he was happy. He and his sister decided to walk home.

On the way, Mike stopped, surprised, at the gate of a small house. He had never noticed the house before, even though he must have walked along this street a hundred times. There was a pumpkin on the porch, but no lights were on.

Mike's sister stopped too.

"Let's go home," Mike said. "We've got enough anyhow."

"You scared?" his sister teased.

SOUNDS CREEPY! WHAT DID THEY DO?

....

....

....

....

STORY #13

STORY #13

Aboy was sitting on the edge of a pier, watching a fish swim below.

"I wish I was that fish," thought the boy. "Then I would swim down deep, and ....

....

That same fish was watching a seagull fly by.

"I wish I was that seagull," thought the fish. "Then I would fly high above the sea, and ....

....

And the seagull was watching the boy on the pier.

"I wish I was that boy," thought the seagull. "Then I would

....

.... WHAT

.... HAPPENED

.... NEXT?

....

....

....

....

STORY #14

NEW STORY!
WHAT'S
GOING ON?

STORY #15

STORY #15

Grandpa is giving Imani an amazing birthday gift—an extra special party. Any kind of party she wants.

There's just one problem. Imani has two great ideas, and she can't decide which one to choose!

"Why don't you make a list?" says Grandpa. "Compare your ideas side by side."

Imani smiles and grabs a pad and pencil.

FILL IN THE LIST!

IDEA: _____

IDEA: _____

WHAT DOES
IMANI DECIDE?

HOW DOES THE
PARTY GO?

Gogorath the demon pirate is having an unlucky day—one of those days when a teeny thing makes a bigger thing happen, which makes an even bigger thing happen, and before you know it there's a mighty ruckus.

The teeny thing at the start of Gogorath's day was that he knocked his jellyfish juice off the breakfast table. Then

....

....

And then ....

....

....

And then ....

....

....

....

....

WHAT WAS THE
MIGHTY RUCKUS?

STORY #17

A lex lives in a mushroom.

It took Addison and her friends eight hours, five hot chocolate breaks, and three changes of dry gloves and socks, but it was finally done — the biggest snowman ever.

Happy and tired, they all went inside for dinner. Midway through her second bowl of spaghetti, Addison heard a *thump thump thump* outside.

She opened the back door to see what was going on. The snowman was gone.

Meanwhile, the snowman was

MAKE A COMIC! DRAW, WRITE, USE SPEECH BUBBLES, COLOR. GO WILD!

KEEP GOING . . .

WHAT ABOUT ADDISON? DOES SHE SEE THE SNOWMAN AGAIN?

This is ...., goddess of the Sun and ....

Now, there are three things you need to know about her.

First, you'd never guess, but she is one thousand years old. Second, she .... And third, she ....

One afternoon she was lying in the park, listening to .... , when ....

STORY #20

Lunch is finished, and Will's hands are washed. It's time to play outside.

Will puts on a jacket and some shoes, opens the front door, and almost runs into . . . an egg!?

A gigantic, colorful egg.

"Whoa!" says Will.

"Whoa," says his dad.

"Whoa," says the egg.

COLOR IN
IF YOU LIKE
☺

STORY #21

WHAT'S INSIDE?
DRAW IT!

STORY #21

Ellie looked for the perfect camping spot while her mom drove slowly through the campground.

"There!" said Ellie, pointing out her mom's side.

"Yeah, there," said her brother, Carlos.

"Agreed, really?" said their mom. "Agreed!" She parked the car.

Ellie jumped out and ran over to the spot. Yes, perfect, she thought. There was ....

....

and ....   **DESCRIBE THE**
                                                                       CAMPING SPOT!

and ....

....

....

They unpacked the car and put up their tent. Carlos looked for good trees for hanging the hammocks, and Ellie went to collect firewood.

Ellie wandered through the light scrub, singing, picking up only the best sticks, when she saw

My New Superpower and Other Stories We Write Together
Copyright © 2020, 2023 by Rick Benger
All rights reserved.

Published by Collins, an imprint of HarperCollins Publishers Ltd

Previously published in a slightly different form as *Once upon a Pancake for Younger Storytellers*
in 2020 by Pfannkuchen Press LLC

First published by Collins in 2023 in this original trade paperback edition

Original illustrations by Maddie Egremont in stories 2, 5, 10, and 14; by Matej Beg in story 4;
and by Daniel Howard in story 7. All other images and adapted images, with the exception of the
original illustrations in stories 3, 8, 15, 19, and 21, are licensed via Shutterstock.

HarperCollins books may be purchased for educational, business,
or sales promotional use through our Special Markets Department.

HarperCollins Publishers Ltd
Bay Adelaide Centre, East Tower
22 Adelaide Street West, 41st Floor
Toronto, Ontario, Canada
M5H 4E3

www.harpercollins.ca

ISBN 978-1-4434-7100-8

Printed and bound in Latvia
PNB 9 8 7 6 5 4 3 2 1

RICK BENGER is the creator of Once upon a Pancake, a series of interactive books with unfinished stories inside. He occasionally writes stories all by himself—a selection of which can be found at rickbenger.com, where you'll also find his newsletter about being a new dad.